Patterns from the Air

T0313580

Contents

Written by Liz Miles

Collins

Deserts

From up high, you can see clear patterns in the land.

In deserts, gusts of wind sweep the sand grains into patterns and hills. Storms can scoop up the sand and drop it in towns.

Scorching hot sun and a lack of rain can crack the land. Trees and shrubs turn brown.

Rainforest

A big river sweeps and twists across the rainforest. This wet habitat is crowded with trees.

This rainforest has been spoilt. The trees
are cut down for wood. They form
a pattern of blacks and browns.

Coast

At the coast, this river sweeps across the plain. Splitting into lots of rivers, it forms a clear brown pattern across the green land.

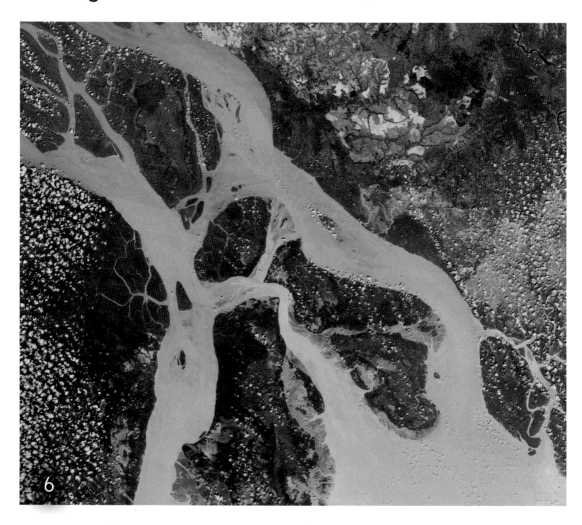

Further along the coast, crashing storms and shifting sands form bright bands.

smooth sands

froth

Crops

Crops of fresh flowers are as bright as a painting!

Farmers will cut them and bring them to the market to sell.

On steep hills, farmers cut flat steps for crops.

Transport

We can see patterns in bright painted trains transporting goods such as food.

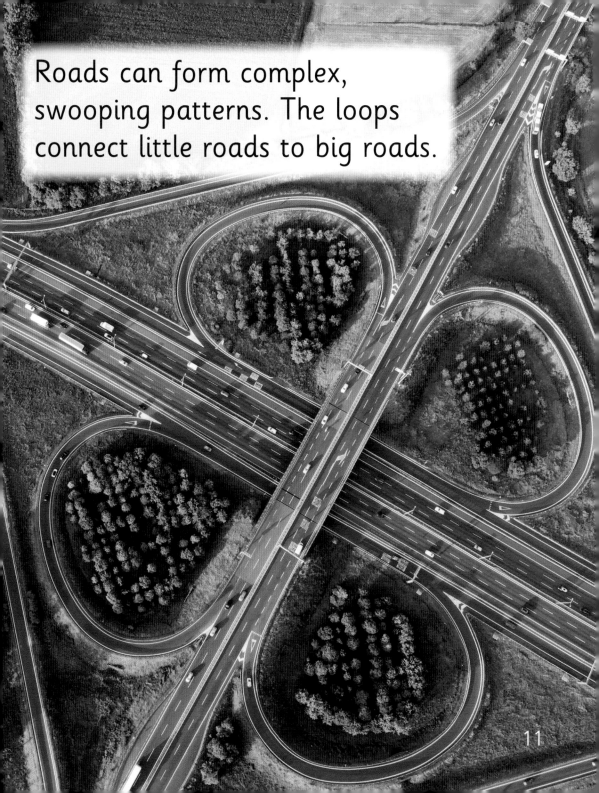

Roads can form complex, swooping patterns. The loops connect little roads to big roads.

Towns

This grid pattern of streets has been well planned. Lots can be crowded in to not much land.

This stunning resort forms a flat, floating tree pattern! You can visit it!

Patterns from the air

🐾 Review: After reading 🐾

Use your assessment from hearing the children read to choose any GPCs, words or tricky words that need additional practice.

Read 1: Decoding

- Write the word **bands** on the board. Discuss its different meanings. (e.g. *music group, strip – elastic band or hat band; strip of colour*) Ask the children to find the word on page 7. Ask: What is its meaning in this sentence? (e.g. *bright bands of colour*)

- Practise sounding out words with adjacent consonants. Ensure they don't miss any sounds:

  p/a/tt/er/n/s   a/c/r/o/ss   t/w/i/s/t/s   f/l/oa/t/i/ng

  o Ask the children to find more words with adjacent consonants to sound out and blend.

- Challenge the children to read a sentence with fluency. Tell them to try to read the words without sounding them out, but they can blend in their heads if they need to.

Read 2: Prosody

- Model reading pages 10 and 11 to the children as if you are a television presenter.

- Challenge the children to take turns to practise reading a page to a partner as if they were a television presenter too. Say: How clear and interesting can you make the information sound?

- Ask children to read out their pages, and discuss what works well, and what emphasis or change of tone might improve the readings.

Read 3: Comprehension

- Talk about what patterns the children might see if they flew over the area where they live. Ask: What tree/road/building patterns might you see?

- Discuss whether all patterns are formed by nature. If necessary point to pages 8–13, where the patterns are made by people.

- Look at pages 14 and 15. Which pattern do the children like best? Can they explain what each **pattern** is made by?

  o Discuss each of the patterns. Ask: Can you see any lines? Do the lines form shapes? Is there just one shape or lots of the same shape?